DECEPTION

FOR DENIS,
who helps me find my good spirit
and my better self

~ Contents ~

CHOPIN FOR THE DYING

VARIATIONS ON A THEME BY CLOZAPINE

BULIMIA IN THE KEY OF DEBUSSY

Préludes Book I

Préludes Book II

Chopin for the Dying

For Jeanne and Rennie Heal

REUNION

see you later I assured
with a squeeze of my hand
before they took you away

simple they said
straightforward
cartilage and bone removed
plastic and metal put in their place

but there were complications
unforeseen reactions
between anesthetic and medication

oh   your knee healed
but your lungs swelled
filled within themselves

bronchiolitis they said
obliterans
organizing pneumonia
boop
deception
their solution to your pain

the dawn was lost you said
in the mist
and I could see it
hear it in the music you played
the Chopin from Majorca
cold and rainy
fog and darkness rolling in

14   the music stopped in the twilight hour
       our golden dreams were nothing
       but coughs   gasps
       air you could not catch

       see you later I whispered
       as you went away
       see you later you choked
       in reply

PRESENTIMENT OF DEATH

they were there in Majorca
the beaks and horns
masks and shadows knocking
with shepherds' crooks on Chopin's door

then his turquoise sky
his ancient palm trees and olives
his wet lapis lazuli sea
were washed away in grey

dead monks prayed once
engraved the damp
walls of his cell with their souls
full of fire
smothered and extinguished

and in your room
you ate cherry pie
even though you always said
it reminded you of organs
and clotting blood
I always made another sort
apple or meringue   coconut or flapper
always until the day you asked
for such red sweetness
between breaths

⟡

THOU ART SO LIKE A FLOWER

rooted in bed
my white lupin
tubes up your nose
and down your throat
anchoring your body
to air

I touch your skin
pale and delicate
a soft crocus
in the spring snow

study the hidden green tulips
of your eyes
buried beneath the weight
of your sleeping lids

your room is a garden
of delivered bouquets
mums and carnations
lemon leaves and myrtle
multicoloured feathers
plucked from an eagle

Chopin floats from the radio
a melodic fragrance for you
pulsating with every breath
of your machine

it's beautiful
this deception of harmony
of nature and science
of flowers that release their scent
with the voices of fairies
sighing under silver bells

to die this way
you whisper
is welcomed

SUFFOCATION

18   only when it is all over
the sitting
the conversing with family and friends
nodding and smiling at the healthy
only then am I free
to gasp and dream
escape from my deception
that you will get better   heal

your skin is pale
as alabaster broken
and spilled of perfume
by the woman at Christ's feet
washed with her tears
dried with her long dark hair

shall I do the same
I who was never
cut out to be a saint
repent of my words
my smiles that reassure
your parents
your children
you

shall I shed such tears
hidden in the depth
of my damp heart

UNCERTAINTY

waxing or waning
I do not know the difference
whether the sun or the moon
is first in the sky
I still see night
illuminated by celestial bodies
moons   planets   stars

the pink times of day
dusk or dawn
I can only tell
by the direction I must face
when I leave you
follow the music
down the hall

coming or going
is hard to determine
the geese and monarchs
en route for home
or flying away
the air under their wings
pumped into currents
for the weak ones to ride

Chopin's thin   pale appearance
made him seem near death yet
he lived
and people thought
he could go on living
that way forever

20 he has
his hollow body now earth
dust under marble stone
his heart a treasure
inside a Warsaw pillar
his thick notes light
as lace in the sky
a ribbon of stars
for us to connect
as this life waxes
and wanes

≻

TOLLING BELLS

we can hear them like a veil
floating down twentieth street
past the pawn shops and bingo halls
those cast metal cathedral cries
to love
to be loved
such happiness
it's divine

they remind us of vows
exchanged when we still had
everything that is most exquisite
this side of heaven
each other
to have
and to hold
while the children slept

for better
or for worse
this is the promised land
this sterile room
these pumps breathing for you
this place of sickness
that stole your health

still
we cherish one another
until death

THE POLISH DANCER

after the preludes
you listen to nocturnes
mazurkas   polonaises
they make you dream

tuxedos and evening gowns
ballrooms and champagne

you were hopeful once
that you would dance
walk like yourself again
but without the pain

robes and slippers
hospital rooms and Demerol

listen you say
to the music
such beauty
deceives the pain

DESPERATION

age made you
and your heart
and your knee
made you retire after forty years in a mine
but golden hours could still be had
with medication and surgery

you went
sat on the bed to undress
to shave your knee
to lie in wait of deliverance
anesthetic
lapis lazuli sleep
was your first relief

after the needle you wandered
wafted along like smoke from a ship's funnel
carried away by the breeze
the doctor's words became
a dreamy soliloquy
meandering
the murmur of an eddy

then you awoke
but could not breathe
pain
a heart attack
would have been easier than this
bronchioloitis obliterans organizing pneumonia
this boop

the doctors can eat simulated butter
and call it popcorn lung if they wish
but there is no curtain on this Betty
no closing credits at the end of the show
this is drowning
suffocating

this is despair

VISION

sometimes the rhythm of your breathing
machine lulls me to sleep
and only your words
little wife Horner
sat in the corner
dreaming of Christmas pie
can make me smile
but I do not open my eyes
for in my dreams it is you
you with good knees and free lungs
you not plums
I pull from that pie

)~

THE NIGHT MOTH

evenings
after days at the hospital
I find my way home
turn the key
greet the silence
with the rebolting of the door

I flutter about
the flashing telephone
the unopened bills
the giant soaker tub you'd thought
would be good for our knees

Epsoms salts and bergamot
water clouding the mirror
I slip in
submerge
hold my breath
until my heart beats
against my ears

THE DRAGON FLY

lying in tandem
is as close as we can get
with the tubes up your nose
and down your throat
our fingers touching
grasping
like yellow emperors
copulating in Majorca
fluttering without the least thought
of death

like us
so many months and years ago
the summer of our love
you would say if you dared
unburden your soul
but your sorrows
your griefs
cannot be expressed in words

had you the knowledge
the strength
you would compose
all the tenderness
the humility of
an unmurmuring regret
of medication and anesthetic
forming bronchial disease
eating our lives

ᒧ

THE DUEL

it was not so much a fight
you said but a misunderstanding
she was tired
disturbed
her children were growing
into their own minds
and Fred
he was
you cannot say anymore
he was sick
of sugared gum water and opium
laxatives   leeches   blood-letting
of always needing the dawn
to find the strength of a new day

I am the same
as both of them
sick   and tired
of waiting for healing ·
recovery
of watching you pale
wither without air
I do not sleep
do not cut my hair
I do not have the strength
to call the salon
to go and sit
chat about the weather
what do I know about the weather
inclement or fair
artificial light surrounds me
most of every day

in Majorca they say God
helps those who get up early
but I cannot throw off my covers
cannot push myself out of bed before
the sun has burned the clouds away
and how somber
how painfully unhappy I feel
later when I see you
my well-rooted lupin
plumped up among the violets
and the watered bouquets

your window overlooks the valley
the leaves are full and green
you do not look out
wish you were there
instead you speak of Sand
the victim of her own heart
the injustice
the pinpricks she suffered
you do not say she was the grain
that disrupted the tranquil lake
that she caused the pebbles
and rocks of friendship
to fall one
by one

my heart is bursting
my head aflame
over your preferential treatment
your lack of sympathy
but I remain silent
sit by your side
read Cabrera Infante and wonder
why his tigers were sad
in Spanish but trapped in English
and then I think of the zoo so long ago
the peacock tails and cockatoos
the clay skin of the elephants
their heavy eyes the size of my palm
in yours and their stream of urine
making us laugh

such summer days are gone now
feces and urine are cause
for daily medical inquiry
no doctor you say
will do me as much good
as you
yet we are trapped
like poor Infante
swallowing wheat in a wheat field

LOSS

look I said holding out the pot of leaves and stems
a tomato plant for our patio
you smiled
your oxygen tank inhaled
bring it here
let me smell
I swallowed and acquiesced
your chest ballooned as you breathed
it smells like life you said
my back turned to you
I cried as I prepared the soil

look you said   pointing every morning
it's grown   and I would smile
rush onto the patio to see the miracle you were seeing
study the stalk for endless moments
lift the leaves and look for signs of growth
stuffed tomatoes
toasted sandwiches
sliced with pepper and salt
your eyes shone as we planned our feasts

like apples
golden delicious or granny smith
the tomatoes were still green when you left
still needed time and sun

when I watered them
I held my face to their leaves
inhaled their green perfume
thought of the ancient Aztecs feeding
the earth with the crimson
sacrifice of life

32 you never saw the tomatoes' flesh
    swell with summer
    turn shades of yellow and orange
    never tasted their juice of captured sun

    now plump and red
    your fruit is heavy
    in my empty hand

FEAR

your pajamas and robe
the prayer book and bible you kept by your bed
the blanket I knit to keep you warm
together in a box marked Heal (our last name
such a wound)

your watch and tie
the cuff links from our tenth anniversary
your stiff white shirt and pinstriped suit
surely folded carefully without wrinkle
in a box passed to me with undertaker's sympathy

all the recordings
the biographies and histories
letters and pencil sketches that kept you
company those many months
closed away like Chopin's heart
in a crypt I will never visit
for fear I will be deceived
by the beauty
of all that was you

﹀

RAINDROPS

there are as many different sounds
you said as there are raindrops
listen
but I could only hear
the rhythmic patter
of falling water as
you told the story
of Valldemossa
Chopin weeping
dreaming reality
while reality became a dream
Fred himself drowned in a lake
icy water
falling
on his breast

such romanticism I thought
is for romantics
I prefer comedy
Gene Kelly laughing at clouds
splashing in puddles
of water and milk
miming in black and white
I love you
I love you
I love you
you rattlesnake
I've never heard
of anything so low
such a beautiful deception
silent film

and the smiles
the twirls
the Technicolor kisses
between Kelly and Reynolds
the fluid tapping of heels and toes
inside satin shoes stained
with blood from inexperienced feet
off set he made her cry
drove her under the piano
until Fred
Astaire said you can dance
you can dance
I'll show you
she was lucky
in his arms

ridi
pagliacci
fall into a passing car
jump out of a frosted cake
throw another in the kisser
these are no shadows on film
but flesh and blood
trying to say something
in the proper setting
an empty stage
transformed
a beautiful sunset
at the pull of a lever
mist from the distant mountains
and they sure look lovely

in the moonlight
all I do now
is dream of you
the day we met
the air we shared
when we kissed
with the dawn
I still go on
the nights we had
the dreams we lived
they're every song
I would ever sing
if my sorrows were turned
to poetry

were my instincts exalted
above twenty-seven years of valentines
hidden in your sock drawer
or the picture of you
placed on the mantle
I would not cry
to feel the empty space
inside our bed
nor the silence
of your breathing machine
were you here to
encourage me
remind me to listen
to the sounds
of the rain

HADES

I play golf   scorpion   pyramid
alone
cook Majorcan paella   tumbet   pumpkin fritters
for one
read Infante   Sand   stories
about the Mayan god who descended
beneath the great mountain to battle
the lords of death
his head cut off
speared and trophy mounted
on the branch of a dead tree
instantly flourishing
with fruit and foliage
it was the world tree   maize
life springing from death
here   spring is
forgetting us

I buy Styrofoam to remember
the night I bumped into you
spilled hot taupe-coloured coffee
on your hand and on your shoes
your acceptance of the napkins
the bumbling apologies I offered
it was my first time at a widows' group
though I'd been alone for years
the picnic we went on at the zoo
the chicken sandwiches I brought
the dripping ice cream we caught
with our tongues
the elephants you remembered
years later with infected lungs
in the shade   you said between breaths
the one who   lifted its leg

and peed
it was the first time
we laughed

months later you asked me
where I wanted to go
for our honeymoon
I said I don't care
I just want to see a lot of ceiling
so we stayed at the Bessborough
for five days and four nights
last night I stared for hours
but I could not find you
anywhere above

~

A SCENE ON THE PLACE
DE NOTRE-DAME DE PARIS

I wander Paris after you're gone
walk past cafés
bars   boulangeries
tourists gawking
at the beauty that blinds
the Parisians pushing their way to work
I am not looking
for statues or towers
but addresses
boulevard Poisonnière
chausée d'Antin
rue Tronchet

here George lived
how delicious
how wonderful
even in spite of irritations
husbands   boredom   heartbreaks
here Fred lived
among mahogany
cabriolets and white gloves
perfume   ivory   smocks
here was beauty
incessant activity
the greatest virtue and
the worst vice

here such art
Delacroix   Monet   Rodin
Hugo   Dumas   Balzac
Piaf
history
saints and royalty
Napoleon and Hitler's boots
marched   beggars killed
wolves and beheaded kings
here Lutèce
the city of light

Paris awakes
before it has slept
lark song and last night's
French techno dance beat
a duet film score to my sleep
shallow and restless
alone in a room with a little balcony
on the boulevard from which I can see
from Montmartre
to the Panthéon

it is here where the martyrs
of history and thought are
Curie   Braille   Moulin
Voltaire   Malraux
their bodies
their hearts
their remains after reposing
elsewhere for centuries
this is where I look
alone at the start of the day

I walk the city
follow the green and blue signs
pause at 9 square d'Orléans
74 rue Chaillot
12 Place Vendôme   think
I should write
draw
take a picture at least
but my fingers struggle
he breathed here
hoped the spring sunshine
would be his best doctor

to the Madeleine
following after him
one hundred and sixty years later
sixteen months after you
the incense is still burning
drifting up like prayer
suffocation and tolling bells
Mozart's *Requiem*
murmuring his farewell
that distant eve
of All Hallow's Eve
they carried him
the prince   the painter   the composer
and the cellist
down the streets
in silence

in Père Lachaise I lay a rose
between the rods of the iron gate
touch him through marble
and six feet of earth
like Fred
my heart is elsewhere

~

SUICIDE

it was slow
bronchioles and alveoli
organizing
intentionally swelling
plugging themselves with tissue
refusing all treatment
doctors
medication
assisted breathing

though your body
was dying away you never
asked why
doesn't he just kill me outright
instead of making me die little
by little
that was my question
sotto voce at your bedside
do you suffer
I asked
you said
no longer

⟩~

HEARTFELT HAPPINESS

〜(44 I met you when I had already learned
that until death do us part
comes quickly   suddenly
in the middle of morning chores
an accident that blows-up
the marriage bond
after only eight years
four children
ten thousand kisses
you'd learned the same lesson yet
there we were
before an altar
making vows
in sickness and in health we said
then kissed and danced
made love in a king-sized bed
lived together longer than we had
with our previous spouses
combined

twenty-five years together you thought
merited a trip
the mountains were close
but it was winter
and we wanted to have sun and rock
so we flew to Majorca
where we could practice our Spanish
winding through the Tramuntanas
we still thought it was love
that could move mountains
birdsong

cowbells and bleating sheep
olive orchards
valleys of pine and oak
in our hotel room
we retraced the Mediterranean coast
on each others' backs
practiced Spanish words for love
between the sheets

the almond blooms
and dragonflies
the monks' roses at the monastery
the memories
became angels of sweetness and goodness
when we returned home
with photographs and aching knees
Horowitz recordings of Chopin
Sand's greatest works
their wings carried us
to doctors and physio
acupuncture and pharmacies
through months of pain
and the shield of ore
that lay hidden in your chest

your first wife taught you
how to care for the sick
how to smile
and talk to doctors   nurses
visitors wondering
how things are
she taught you
a riddle of what's green on the outside

and yellow on the inside
if you want to know   *espera*
wait
es pera
it's a pear
she taught you   *esperar*
to hope
I never learned this
even now

~

FUNERAL MARCH

every step behind you
wet leaves cake my soles

you liked fall best
the golden poplars
the sound of copper leaves
like crumpled paper beneath your feet
the smell of earth
composting squash and pumpkin seeds

I follow
your casket leads

it passed too quickly
that golden season
the poplars are empty and bare

⟩~

SUNDAY

48   physical healing
the doctors said
was impossible
they could do nothing
but ease your pain
how   I never knew
since you had grown old
before your time
before you had become
tired of passion
or hopelessly disillusioned

sixty's not old
we joked when you retired
if you're a rock
or fire
or the sea
but it became that way
when you couldn't dance
or walk
or breathe
then life was long
even with the garden filled
with birds and honeysuckle

lonicera stems
relieve respiratory tract infections
inhibit bacteria
soothe inflammation
but you had need for more
than relieving heat
clearing toxicity

inducing dreams of love
and running under broken arches
summoning witches
to their sabbath merry-making
easing pain

nothing
in that room
between the cliffs of life
and the sea of eternity
was more melancholy
than the steep slopes
the varied tints of holm-oak
carob trees   pine
blending into thick arbors
unfathomable depths of greenery
that only you could see
after the nurses passed

I know the trees
don't complain of the wind
that batters them
nor the earth of the mountains
which crush it   but
with eighteen months of doctors
pills and monitors
eighteen months of rosary beads
clicking in symphony with your breath
was all I could do
the only tincture I had
to heal

༄

IMPATIENCE

50   although extremely beautiful
the flower book says the modest
touch-me-nots are
quite susceptible to disease
bacterial   fungal   parasitic
and even viral
such a deception to see
the fuschias and pinks
the orange and violet brown
when they are in bloom

I planted them for our anniversary
fifty teardrops covered
with a sprinkling of earth
then waited
dealt cards for solitaire
flower garden patience
laid the cards upright
to make my flower beds
kept sixteen for my bouquet
pulled the aces for foundation heaps

it passed the time
without too much thought
the clicks and rubs of lavender
cards from Harrah's filling the silence
when my garden is stacked
again and again
I visit Sir Tommy
the Yukon   Bristol
stare at red and black
until my patience
or eyesight wears out

sitting on Mary's knee
the child Jesus wished the world
could see her eyes
and with the stretch of his hand
blue forget-me-nots flowered
had I such power
I'd have made us
honeysuckle and hazel
growing flowers entwined
for night moths and butterflies

ﻼ

A PLEASURE BOAT

you bought me Spanish books
on dragonflies and Majorcan history
in the bookstore of the cruise ship

I bought you sun block
and flowered cotton shirts
that you did not wear until
we came home
and you had the surgery
and the boop set in

you said the shirts reminded you
of our hot days in Majorca
and the lapis lazuli sea
my lips darned by dragonflies
I did not say
they reminded me of the cold
that had settled in our bed

I sleep now
ignore the books
the photo albums and flowered shirts
I no longer have
the most beautiful things
here beside me

THE STORM

simplicity is the final achievement
after having conquered all difficulties
after having played a huge quantity of notes
it is simplicity that emerges
with all its charm
as the final seal of art
it is not an easy thing

I have found a misplaced book
between the ultimate book of card games
and if life is a game
these are the rules
like a serpent swallowing a rabbit whole
at the piano with Chopin
opens in my hands
black and white words
that hold the key to understanding
simplicity is the final achievement

it is all luck
the deceptions of science
cartilage and bone or
plastic and metal
after the scar heals
no one knows
unless you can't walk
can't breathe
no one knows
you can't die without
having conquered all difficulties

Fred's left hand
plastered and preserved
photographed on page six
strong   chiseled
manicured for making music
this hand I reach for
hold

yet I resist the dream
the desire for deliverance
after having played a huge quantity of notes
I need some noise
I have heard nothing but pianissimo
since you have gone
the brush of cards
the whisper of pages turning in books
silence
I can shout
at the top of my voice
still silence
simplicity that emerges

backgammon and honeymoon whist
have given way
to solitaire
day or night
even with strategy
it's still luck that counts
moves the cards
builds the foundations
this is widowhood
with all its charm

all this mingles
with the songs of nightingales
and the fragrance of roses
drying in the silence
of flower garden patience
no one is listening to me
but I am listening to myself
were I at the piano
maybe I would be as bold
as the final seal of art

I have found
it is all luck
Fred's left hand
my palm in yours
I need some noise
backgammon and honeymoon whist
shadows on film
all this mingles
with the lesson
it is not an easy thing

♪

Variations on a Theme by Clozapine

THEME

people compose for many reasons
to become immortal
because the pianoforte happens to be open
because they want to become millionaires

people compose for many reasons
to become immortal
because of the praise of friends
because they have looked into a pair of beautiful eyes

they have seen the hands of a girl dance
felt them entwine in theirs
touched them softly against their lips
placed them to their fiery cheek

they have seen the hands of a girl dance
heard her music after she has gone
needed to converse with her
exist with her in sound

they have made music in their minds
they have made music in the mist
on warmed summer stone
under twinkling night sky

people compose for many reasons
to become immortal
because the pianoforte happens to be open
for no reason whatsoever

♪

VARIATION I

people compose for many reasons
to become immortal
because the pianoforte is an intimate orchestra
because they want to speak without words

people compose for many reasons
because paper and ink are in front of them
because a nut tree stands greenly in front of the house
spreading its fragrant branches into the air

they have touched the pale blossoms
like a caressing gentle wind
heard them whisper
paired two by two

a nut tree stands greenly in front of the house
its blossoms incline their tender heads to kiss
their breath is in my lungs
their perfume is in the air

the blossoms whisper of a maiden
who thinks all day and all night
of something she does not know
such a soft song whisper

people compose to become immortal
in the rustle of leaves
the whispers of hoping and yearning
the smiles of sleep and dream

)~

VARIATION II

people compose because the piano happens to be open
to their soul   to their pain
to the world in which they live
their heaven in which they float

people compose because the piano is open
to whispers heard in the trees
while others sleep
dream of maidens and grooms

seen in the dim light
we seem like ordinary people
with ordinary lives
but we are more than lovers
jobs and ambition
we are living
the most beautiful deception
Clozapine can offer
sameness
until the voices sing
to me again

I compose because the piano is open
a grave into which I can cast
eternally my grief   it is my rest
my peace

it makes me worthy
raises me above myself
it is my good spirit
my better self

⁊~

VARIATION III

people compose for many reasons
because they want to become millionaires
because of the praise of friends
because there is a boy there on the threshold

why are you standing there
lovely boy
be my barman
so every glass will be tasty and light

be my barman so every note will sound
will rise above these whispers
of the boors who bring me wine
so roughly and unkind

you will not throw it down
that jug of music and song
so roughly in front of me
and make it grow cloudy in the glass

you will let me make music
in my mind
you will let me make music
from my soul

you understand
people compose for many reasons
because they have had no wine
because they grow cloudy behind the glass

~

VARIATION IV

people love for many reasons 63 ∂⁓
to become immortal
because their heart happens to be open
because they have heard sounds that beguile the heart

people love for many reasons
to become immortal
because their heart can still nurture a hope
because they have looked into a pair of beautiful eyes

depthless pools of stars
through which my joys and agonies
have flown away
in night and wind

in my delusions   my hallucinations
I know you always
cross the distance
to which you have dedicated your life

we make love in our minds
we make love in satin beds
on flowering summer stone
veiled by night sky

people love for many reasons
but I love
for only
one

⁓

VARIATION V

people compose for many reasons
because the pianoforte happens to be open
because they want to become millionaires
because of the praise of friends
because they have looked into a pair of beautiful eyes
for no reason whatsoever
if only because through it they win
hours of self-forgetfulness in a world of sound

I compose for many reasons
I have seen hands dance
have felt the joy of creation
of a religious without religion
when he sees a flower
so pure and fair and bright
and I have had a melancholy yearning
steal over me at your sight

I work to win both the heart and flesh
to become immortal in you
I work for no reason whatsoever
but great pleasure
the joy of creation
I compose for many reasons
to win both the heart and flesh
to become immortal
in a world of sound

~

VARIATION VI

people compose for many reasons
to converse when their lover is gone
because they drink alone
because no one sets a limit

people compose for many reasons
to feel their fingers entwine with another's
because their hands cannot speak
because they have their own thoughts to think

they have seen their hands curl
watched them grow powerless
like a religious without religion
refraining from his wafers

I have seen my hands curl
felt my fingers seize
when placed on ivory
and numbly touched to skin

I have made music in my mind
I have made music in my room
no one sets a limit
on a blank sheet of paper

I compose for many reasons
to converse with others
because my hands cannot speak
because I have my own thoughts to think

𝄐

VARIATION VII

people compose for many reasons
to become immortal
because they want to speak without words
because paper and ink are in front of them
because the gods have taught them
with ivory and double pan flute
to communicate the dots and lines
they have heard in their dreams

composing gives great pleasure
nothing surpasses this joy of creation
through it one wins hours of self-forgetfulness
where one lives in a world of sound
where rest is living
from the outside in
to the marrow of one's bones

composing gives silence voice
amidst the cacophony
of whispers and sighs
I feel your sense
lovingly you seem to say
that you are always beside me
melody must still be formed
shaped in the world of dreams

love makes music for many reasons
to become immortal
because the heart is open
because it wants to be on the lips of millions
because of the praise of gods
because it has looked into a pair of beautiful eyes
love makes music for many reasons
and no reason whatsoever

people compose for many reasons
to converse
because the pianoforte compels them
because they cannot do otherwise
people compose for many reasons
to speak
because of the past
because they have looked into their soul

they have seen their own hands dance
watched themselves grow into genius
written notes like a religious without religion
offered them like holy wafers

they have seen their own hands dance
felt their fingers seize in harmonic desire
placed them on ebony
touched their distorted joints to polished wood

they have made music in their minds
they have made music in hospital rooms
no one sets a limit
on a blank sheet of paper

people compose for many reasons
to become voiced
because the pianoforte compels them
because they cannot do otherwise

I compose this for no reason
but to make you immortal
because my heart happens to be yours
because you are a genius of heart and sound

~68   I compose this for no reason
       but to make us immortal
       because we are composer and interpreter
       melody and hands
       the music our love creates
       in dots and lines
       there is no greater gift
       from you
       or me

       ~

~(Bulimia in the Key)~ of Debussy

PRÉLUDES

Book I

DANCERS OF DELPHI

slow and solemn
seated on my piano bench
calmly held together
my fingers firm
as rubber   good
for pianissimos and jabbing
the back of my throat
I utter the music Claude heard
in the movement of waters
the play of curves in the breeze

softly Agamedes'
Trophonius' words in the foreground
          know thyself
          nothing in excess
messages from greedy hands
snatching up the treasury
          do as you wish for six days
          then   for the good of those around you
          die on the seventh
that too is my prophecy

caught in the snare
I would also cut my head
or fingers   or colon
to hide the secrets of food
and drink for a whole generation
consumed and evacuated in one night
only the oracle knows how much
has to be explored
discarded
before reaching the naked flesh
of feeling

⟆

VOILES

74   sails
or veils
I do not know
any more than moderate
caressing
how to know when
I am nothing
more than a wretched atom
hurled around by this cataclysm
what I'm doing seems
so miserably petty
watching numbers on a scale
adjusting the golden ratio
of food ingested
over food expelled
equals food digested
I should be searching
for the symphonic formula which fits our time
for proof that asteroids pummeled the moon
I should join the celestial police
survey the gap between Jupiter and Mars
that the Lord Architect

         filled with fluid particles
         dwarfs and asteroids
         dust and Debussy
             floating iron
             pulled by an orbiting moon in space
       like a sail in the sea
       a slide of stars
       brought to the fore
       in softness

then I could
return to music and decency
regain a hold of myself
of all the beauty
which has not ceased to exist
despite my oblivion
and my deceptions

~

        animated
        as lightly as possible
this is me while others sleep
cupboards
packages
the fridge
crumbs and stickiness
the kitchen is an open field
for me to blow over

I should be
practicing   making music

Claude calls me
tells me people come to it
to melody
to seek oblivion
I know but
is that a better form
of deception than this
       a little   held back

I tremble

SOUNDS AND PERFUMES
MINGLE IN THE EVENING AIR

now comes
the nightly act
a wave of glistening
resonances behind the stage
I purge

exhale
like a censer
the food   the harmonies
pass between our fingers and mouths
the need for empty intestines
binds us

Claude would
call it nasty
full of painful after-
effects and robbed digestion time
cancer

tender
I say   pungent
a melancholy heart
the emptiness of deception
of food

holding
back more and more
the truth of what I do
is sound and perfume turning in
the air

~ 78   a distant horn call
         still further and more restrained
         Claude's hands slip from mine

            ~

THE HILLS OF ANACAPRI

what shall I release   let vibrate
to allow myself to be buoyant
lively enough to deceive the music
make it believe that I am
joyous   free as a popular song

after cookies and milk of magnesia I am
afraid the only release will be my guts

I would like to run away
roam the hills of Anacapri   float
into the Grotta Azzurra   find myself
the truth lying in luminous blue
between this rapture and this slander

~

FOOTPRINTS IN THE SNOW

slowly and sadly
these dots of ink resonate
the depth of my heart
a frozen rhythm for Claude
who walked with me
through frosted gardens
to January piano lessons
at the end of the lane
in front of ivory
our hands thawed
my footprints melted
left puddles on the floor
now   I slow down
hold back
lose Claude's hands
in this eternal winter
looming long before us
I was to play
the prints he left in the snow

oh   if I could return to summer days 81 ∂~
tender and lush
my small hand humid in his
cold vanilla ice cream melting
in our mouths
but   this sweet confection buries me
slowly and sadly
still I yield to it
those days are but a sad dear longing
getting softer the farther I trudge
and as I disappear
into the snow
his dots of ink
resonate the depth
of my heart
slowly
dying away

~

WHAT THE WEST WIND SAW

~(82   my ashen complexion and my hands
         seized by a frail trembling
         are not causes for restlessness   concern
         as they were for Claude

         they are jarring gusts of chords brought out in anguish
         as I sit on my porcelain throne between
         takes of cupcakes and cd tracks
         which of these   recording or shitting

         would he have preferred
         such glamourous things these replacements
         for beauty of style
         the west wind carries

              ~

THE GIRL WITH THE FLAXEN HAIR

I still remember
a time when lark song was free
calm and sweet

without measure
like summer sun moving
without heaviness across the sky
it murmurs

now it leaves me to lose myself
the most beautiful
deception of all

⟆

THE INTERRUPTED SERENADE

it begins moderately
animated
like a guitar prelude
to a fridge-lit evening
precise and fleeing consumption
of all that is gemlike and musical

the strumming of throat and intestines
is expressive and beseeching
lessened only by the expulsion
of absurd and chimerical

and what's more incomprehensible combinations
of Chinese food   ice cream   chocolate
poptarts   cereal   muffins
cookies   carrots   candies   fried chicken

these are my cigarettes
my last consolations
clenched in my round   supple   plump hands
hanging heavy on my arms

I move freely
hold back
rage with anger
suddenly quiet down
then rage again
until calm returns once more

such deception
I feel robbed
stifled by barren traditions
that insist on complete digestion
I envy Claude's cut colon

this would allow me to interrupt
the nightly serenade
where there is no theory
and pleasure is the law

⁊

THE SUNKEN CATHEDRAL

86   it is a dawn mistaken for a sunset
        this deep calm
        this harmonious haze
        this legend
        I am the princess who was never
        cut out to be a saint
        corrupt and selfish   I
        open the door to the storm
        to flood the fires of my soul

        with an expression that becomes more
        grandiose   I sink while Claude rises
        from the damp ruins of my life
        like an echo   I am
        parts of all that came before me
        music   food   intestines
        oblivion disguised as art
        I am the most beatiful deception of all

PUCK'S DANCE

playful
and light   it danced into my life
when I was toiling in
factories of
nothing

victim
of my uncultivated state
only food could hold me
one deception
after

many
while I tried to follow Claude's steps
in celestial orbits
around the world
of sound

I was
nothing   merely the instrument
of some destiny that knew
how to hold back
the moon

purging
kept me like him   my asteroid
flying between the laws
of pleasure and
of war

ᷡ

MINSTRELS

they are never moderate
the binges   nor the purges
but nervous   excitable   humourous too
a sinister practical joke
an extended portrayal
of human feelings
once the burning stops
and my guts return to their places

they are mocking punch lines
always on the beat

the whimsical illusionist
prancing about the screen
pulling bats and skeletons from the air

teachers and critics drumming
modulate   modulate
Claude's dry smile   why
theory does not exist
you only have to listen
pleasure

pleasure
is the law
that runs the show
of this life

PRÉLUDES

Book II

FOG

equal and light
the desire
to eat
to hide beneath gossamer clouds the colour of my soul
      iron-grey
      hard and rigid
      hueless
      without reflection
the desire to tear
the veils off idols
of beauty and sound
of digestion and deception
underneath there is nothing but effacement
a sad skeleton
almost nothing more

DEAD LEAVES

slow and melancholic
gently held by no one
but Claude
his music
the silence between the notes

my decay is gravely expressive
a secret brought out piano pianissimo
my hollow face
melted wax and ash
no light of fever

but gloom
always there
like autumn colours hidden by green
exposed at death

THE DOOR OF THE VINE

in the rhythm of Habanera
with sudden contrasts between
extreme violence and soft passion
I change like the rock at Alhambra
silver by starlight
gold in sunlight
a pearl set

in emeralds
chlorophyll canopies above trunks of stone
an arched passageway
to the tower of justice
the courts of lions and myrtles
power and strength
courage I wish I could bathe in
surely Claude

would find something to do with this
if he were here
rather than orbiting around the sun with Seki's 3-8-5-1
while I myself extinguish

⌒

THE FAIRIES ARE
EXQUISITE DANCERS

quickly and lightly
the food enters my mouth
passes teeth   tongue   esophogus
slides to where it is merely the instrument of some destiny
            digestion
            absorption
            defecation
but I try to free it
from barren traditions that stifle it
force it onto my body
into fat

I know it's absurd   chimerical
incomprehensible

cobweb threads of cells
spun into tissue   glands
entrails that can be cut   patched
paralysed
worn down
bled daily over time

still we aspire
Claude and I
to the freedom which nature
has given us   sylphs of ebony
playing upon the spider's wire of
good food and good wine

we are soulless but mortal
hopeful that we shall remain a deception
lest we become utilitarian
sad as a factory
eating and shitting for nothing
but life

ﻝ

HEATHER

calm
the distant mauve sea
the lark when I was golden
singing of love while I gorged

myself listening to music
in the studio at the end of the lane
before ice cream confections

impacted me   caused me
constipation   bloating   pain
loss of all function
normal to those who can excrete

GENERAL LAVINE——ECCENTRIC

in the movement of a cakewalk
I pay homage to Chopin   Bach
Ed   the theatre man made of wood
once my guts return music should
humbly seek to please like brown bock

aged through winter   drunk while we talk
of colostomy and food locks
that heal us   lead us as they should
in the movement

of food and waste   my body's chock
against the edge of health   life's clock
ticking Ed's do-dah   do-dah   should
I care to listen his song would
show me how to fly like a roc
lost in movement

THE TERRACE OF
MOONLIGHT AUDIENCES

under the moonlight
Claude hunts for neither pen
nor light   yet still
he beckons me to my rest
my peace
he alone makes me worthy
raises me above myself
eating   shitting
deception no longer beautiful
my cut side
my excrement in a bag

ninety years after death
he is my good spirit
my better self
his voice   mine
still audible in the moonlight
when we listen

waxing or waning
I do not know the difference
whether the sun or the moon is first
in the sky I still see Debussy   Alhambra
all the asteroids and stars I need
to understand that there is nothing in the moonlight
no passing figures or things without shadows
no deceptions to confine this piece to the page
nor my eyes' waters
to their sobbing sprays

UNDINE

playfully

with a little humour aimed at good old Clementi
he snuck
that bearded man with walking stick and cigarettes
into my lessons at the end of the lane

Doctor Gradus
Jimbo   the dolls   the little shepherd
Golliwogg
shimmering
all of them
murmuring
as best to drown the sound   the sea

soulless
I could not impose myself upon the music
any more than upon the rules of digestion
it was necessary to abandon myself
let the music   the food   do as it would with me
make me a nymph
a water sprite looking for redemption   mortality
among the flows
of dots and lines   blood
excrement through a hole
I'm like him now
my Claude
my prince

⌇.

HOMAGE TO S. PICKWICK
ESQ. P.P.M.P.C.

100   proof of the careful attention   indefatigable assiduity
      and nice discrimination .
involved in making such decisions as
    cutting myself   pulling my insides outside in order to
    keep myself from pain and total obliteration
    while victories over my true self are won day by day
    inside my gastro-intestinal tract
converts into dazzling brilliancy that obscurity in which I
kept every one but Claude

CANOPIC JARS

very calm and sweetly sad
ancient alabaster jars hold internal organs   the embalmed
we live through nasty moments and painful after-effects
our bodies are preserved

ancient alabaster jars hold internal organs   the embalmed
we are cut   gutted   sewn
our bodies are preserved
we may now eat and drink as normal

we are cut and gutted and sewn
we live through nasty moments and painful after-effects
we may now eat and drink as normal
very calm and sweetly sad

~

ALTERNATING THIRDS

102   it has become an open air art
       this digestion   boundless as the elements
       the wind   the sky   the sea

       still I cannot help but see
       myself as a grotesque art
       plugged and sliced and plucked   the elements

       of my being pulled outside their interior element
       my compulsion still left to roar like the sea
       will it never be shut in and become an academic art

       a mortal art stayed by elements more powerful than the sea

FIREWORKS

Function
can be restored
despite oblivion
and deception   beauty can still
exist

I wish
for a freedom
in eating   capable
of conveying the enigma
of food

Rocs lost
in movement fly
with prey caught up between
the clutches of their toes   drop them
to death

Equal
light and distant
the processes of need
a golden ratio of input
output

Without
measures of self
Claude   Alhambra orbit
the solar plane   shattered pieces
as one

Outside
insides become
the truth of what I do
sounds and perfumes turning   rising
in air

Rapture
slander are still
found in luminous blue
as food and digestion return
music

Know how
much has to be
explored and discarded
before reaching the naked flesh
of truth

Still Claude's
dots of ink are
resolved on victory
together we march on
unsheathed   march on

Author's Note

A few years ago, while seated at my piano preparing for
a conservatory examination, my mind began to wander
from the dots and lines on the pages in front of me, and
I began composing poetry, there, in my studio, while my
fingers moved about the keys. After repeated attempts to
focus my attention back to music, I concluded that the
only solution was to follow the muses and hope that once I
indulged them I would be able to return to my Petrof and
practice in a more deliberate and effective manner. This
was not the case, for neither Calliope nor Euterpe have
ever seemed willing to let me go. As a result, I have com-
bined two long threads of my life—music and writing—
together for this collection.

"When you get music and words together," pop singer
Bryan Ferry once noted, "that can be a very powerful
thing," and although the poems included here are not
set to music like the lyrics of a Roxy Music song, they
are, nonetheless, a combination of music and words, of
elements of musical scores and various narratives: the
poems quote freely from the composers who have inspired
them and weave their performance indications, lieder and
personal letters into the narrative, and the forms of the
poetry are linked to the compositions they embody—a
five-part song, for example, becomes a cinquain, or a
piece in ternary form becomes a tritina, or the number
of lines in a poem equals the number of measures in
the music. Despite this symbiosis, the poems are neither
anagrams nor depictions of the music. They are, rather,
explorations of the themes and subjects of the music in all
its many facets: written, preformed, heard, imagined, and
remembered.

While combining music and words together may be powerful, I realise it may also discourage readers who are not familiar with the musical compositions or composers involved in the poetry. This, however, need not be the case; understanding and appreciation of the poems included here can be had without delving into such details, for poetry, like music, must never, as Claude Debussy would say, "be shut in and become an academic art." Nonetheless, the following contextualization and the Notes & Sources section at the end of this book will assist readers who wish to familiarize themselves with the musical aspects of the poems, and, of course, many recordings exist and can satisfy readers who wish to hear the soundtrack while they read.

Frédéric Chopin and his music provide the narrator of "Chopin for the Dying" and her husband comfort and solace as the latter is overcome by Bronchiolitis Obliterans Organizing Pneumonia (BOOP). The circumstances of Chopin's life—his Tuberculosis, his relationship with George Sand (Aurore Dupin), his death and burial—and the romantic Majorcan tales surrounding the creation of his *24 Préludes, Opus 28* are woven together with the couple's experiences of hospitalization, marriage and music.

"Variations on a Theme by Clozapine" explores love, music and Schizophrenia through the knitting together of a famous quote by Robert Schumann, lyrics from his lieder, and the love letter of a composer taking Clozapine for his psychosis. Thematically, the poem parallels the married life of Clara and Robert Schumann as well as the latter's mental illness. Structurally, the poem follows the form of Clara's composition, "Variations on a Theme by Robert Schumann, Opus 20," which was a gift of love and admiration offered to her husband shortly before his definitive mental breakdown.

"Bulimia in the Key of Debussy" reveals a pianist's affinity for Claude Debussy, his music, his person, his story.

The section sets the gritty details of laxative abuse, rectal cancer and colostomies against the poetic and imaginative titles of Debussy's *Préludes* and the many artistic works that inspired them. Debussy's descriptive performance instructions and personal letters are woven throughout the narrative as well thereby creating fugue-like poems.

Together, the three sections create a full and complete programme of poetry that will transport the reader through time—from the 1800s back to ancient Greece and forward to the present. It will travel from place to place, from Paris to Saskatoon and Majorca, to hospital beds and concert stages. It will link and twist and turn fact and fiction, myth and reality in order to create a most beautiful deception.

Notes & Sources

CHOPIN FOR THE DYING

The poems in this section are set to Frédéric Chopin's
24 Préludes, Opus 28, most of which were written during
his winter in Majorca, Spain (1838–39) while he suffered
from poor pulmonary health due to Tuberculosis. He did
not name the preludes; the titles used here were the ones
given by nineteenth century pianist Hans von Bülow. A
formal relationship between the musical score and the
poems exists in the equation of one mesure of music
equals one line of verse.

I consulted a variety of sources while working on these
poems, but the ones listed below were of particular help
and provided the material for the quotes:

Atwood, William G. *The Lioness and the Little One: The Liaison of George
Sand and Frédéric Chopin.* New York: Columbia University Press,
1980.

Atwood, William G. *The Parisian Worlds of Frédéric Chopin.* New
Haven: Yale University Press, 1999.

Hinson, Maurice. *At the Piano With Chopin.* Van Nuys: Alfred
Publishing Co., 1986.

Palmer, Willard A. "The Preludes of Frederic Chopin Opus
28." *Chopin Preludes for the Piano,* 2nd edition. Van Nuys: Alfred
Publishing Co., 1992.

"Basilique du Sacré-Coeur, Paris." <http://en.wikipedia.org/wiki/
Sacré-Cœur,_Paris>.

"Frédéric Chopin." <http://en.wikipedia.org/wiki/
Frédéric_Chopin>.

"Preludes (Chopin)." <http://en.wikipedia.org/wiki/
Preludes_(Chopin)>.

"Prelude, Op. 28, No. 15 (Chopin)." <http://en.wikipedia.org/wiki/
Prelude_Op._28,_No._15>.

Singin' in the Rain. Dir. Gene Kelly and Stanley Donen. Perf. Gene
Kelly, Donald O'Connor and Debbie Reynolds. 1952. Turner
Entertainment Co., 2002. DVD.

VARIATIONS ON A THEME
BY CLOZAPINE

In 1853, pianist and composer Clara Schumann composed a set of piano variations, "Variations on a Theme by Robert Schumann, Opus 20," for her husband's birthday. The following year, Robert tried to commit suicide. His attempt led to his confinement in a mental institution and to speculation over the nature of his problems. Scholars have suggested Schizophrenia, Depression, Bipolar Disorder and Tertiary Syphilis, but there is no consensus. For the sake of the narrative of the poem, I have followed the theory that Schumann suffered from Schizophrenia. The book *The Center Cannot Hold: My Journey Through Madness* (Hyperion Books, 2007) by Elyn R. Saks was most helpful in understanding this illness and offered profound insight into Schizophrenic psychosis.

The poetic variations are based on a Robert Schumann quotation: "People compose for many reasons: to become immortal; because the pianoforte happens to be open; because they want to become a millionaire; because of the praise of friends; because they have looked into a pair of beautiful eyes; for no reason whatsoever." They also quote from his collection of lieder *Myrthen, Opus 25*, whose English translations I found on "The Lied, Art Song, and Choral Texts Page" (http://www.recmusic.org/lieder/).

Structurally, the poem follows the form of Clara Schumann's musical composition with one line of verse representing one measure of music. For the sake of esthetics, many of the repeats have not been reproduced.

The various quotations of both Robert and Clara Schumann used in the poem are quips that are often found in biographical materials, including entries about the composers on www.essentialsofmusic.com and www. classicalarchives.com, and quote-mills such as www. thinkexist.com. Quotations and biographical information were also found in the following books:

Reich, Nancy B. *Clara Schumann: The Artist and the Woman*. Ithaca:
    Cornell University Press, 1985.
Schumann, Eugenie. *The Schumanns and Johannes Brahms—The Memoir
    of Eugenie Schumann*. Freeport: Books for Libraries Press, 1927.
Worthen, John. *Robert Schumann: Life and Death of a Musician*. New
    Haven: Yale University Press, 2007.

BULIMIA IN THE KEY OF DEBUSSY

Claude Debussy published two books of *Préludes* for the
piano in 1910 and 1913. Many of the works were com-
posed as musical responses to art—myth (Delphi, Ondine),
literature (Verlaine, Beaudelaire, Loti, Puaux), visual art
(Arthur Rackham illustrations), theatre performance (Ed
Lavine, Charlie Chaplin) and architecture (Alhambra
Palace)—and often quoted from other musical sources
(*God Save the King, Au Clair de la lune, La Marsaillaise*). In the
scores of his *Préludes*, Debussy included many descriptive
performance markings, which I have incorporated into
the text of many of the poems.

In 1915, Claude Debussy underwent a colostomy for
rectal cancer. The same operation can sometimes be re-
quired by people who abuse laxatives to such a point that
colon function is severely hindered, and bleeding, pain
and compaction of waste occurs. The operation may be
reversible in some situations. For Debussy, it was not, as
it was the only treatment option available to prolong his
life, which ended during a German bombardment of his
home city of Paris in 1918.

Maurice Hinson's editions of the *Préludes* were a
valuable resource to me while writing these poems. The
relationship between musical form, as analyzed by Hinson,
and poetic form is outlined in the following tables.

BOOK I

Prelude	*Musical Form*	*Poetic Form / Relationship*
Dancers of Delphi	Ternary	3 stanzas (mes:lines)
Voiles	5 part song	mes:lines, words, lines
The Wind Over the Plains	Ternary with Intro & Coda	Ternary with Intro & Coda (mes:words)
Sounds and Perfumes Mingle in the Evening Air	5 part song with coda	Crown Cinquain with Hokku
The Hills of Anacapri	Ternary	3 mathematical stanzas (mes:words)
Footprints in the Snow	2 part song with coda	2 stanzas (mes:lines) with mini envoi
What the West Wind Saw	Ternary	3 stanzas (mes:words)
The Girl With the Flaxen Hair	Ternary	3 stanzas of 13 words (words:mes)
The Interrupted Serenade	7 part song	7 mathematical stanzas mes:words
The Sunken Cathedral	Binary	2 stanzas (mes:words)
Puck's Dance	5 part song	Reverse Crown Cinquain
Minstrels	5 part song	5 stanzas (mes:words)

BOOK II

Prelude	Musical Form	Relationship
Fog	5 part song	(mes:words)
Dead Leaves	Ternary	3 stanzas (mes:words)
The Door of the Vine	Ternary	3 stanzas (mes:words)
The Fairies are Exquisite Dancers	5 part song	5 stanzas (mes:words)
Heather	Ternary	Ternary (3mes of 17 words)
General Lavine—Eccentric	Rondo	Rondeau
The Terrace of Moonlight Audiences	3 part song	3 stanzas (mes:lines, words, lines)
Undine	Ternary	3 stanzas (mes:words, words, lines)
Homage to S. Pickwick Esq. P.P.M.P.C.	Ternary	Acrostic
Canopic Jars	Ternary + codetta	Pantoum
Alternating Thirds	Ternary	Tritina
Fireworks	Ternary (Intro, 3 parts, Coda)	Acrostic Crown Cinquain

In addition to quoting from Debussy's performance markings, I also quote from the following sources:

Code, David J. *Claude Debussy*. London: Reaktion Books Ltd., 2010.

Djupdal, Karstein. *A Piano Method by Claude Debussy*. Web. 11 April 2011.

Fulcher, Jane F., ed. *Debussy and His World*. Princeton: Princeton University Press, 2001.

Hinson, Maurice. *Debussy Préludes, Book 1 For the Piano*. Van Nuys: Alfred Publishing Co., 1992.

Hinson, Maurice. *Debussy Préludes, Book 2 For the Piano*. Van Nuys: Alfred Publishing Co., 1992.

114

Lessure François and Roger Nichols, eds. *Debussy Letters*. London: Faber and Faber, 1987.

Nichols, Roger. *Debussy Remembered*. London: Faber and Faber, 1992.

Nichols, Roger. *The Life of Debussy*. Cambridge: Cambridge University Press, 1998.

Roberts, Paul. *Claude Debussy*. London: Phaidon Press Ltd., 2008.

"Claude Debussy Quotes." <http://www.thinkexist.com/quotes/claude_debussy>.

"Main Belt Asteroid." <http://en.wikipedia.org/wiki/Main_belt_asteroid>.

Acknowledgements

Earlier versions of some of these poems appeared in the following publications: *Crave It: Writers and Artists Do Food* (Red Claw Press), *Other Voices*, *The Dawntreader*, *The Prairie Journal*, and *Tempo*.

The poems included in "Chopin for the Dying" had a first incarnation as the poetry component of my MA in Creative Writing Final Portfolio, *Two Roads in a Yellow Wood*, at Lancaster University under the tutelage of Michelene Wandor. Many thanks to her for her encouragement and to Jane Draycott, also at Lancaster University, for planting the first seeds for the poems. Thank you as well to Alberta Scholarship Programs for the support provided through an Arts Award for Career Development, which helped me pursue my studies.

Thank you to Nicholas Mather and Jenna Greig and every one at Rabid Marmot Productions who worked to stage "Variations on a Theme by Robert Schumann," a duet version of "Variations on a Theme by Clozapine." Hats off to C.J. Rowen and Jaimi Reese who brought to life Rob and Claire.

Thank you to Peter Midgley at the University of Alberta Press who was excited about this book from the beginning and never stopped championing it.

Thank you to the many teachers I've had over the years: because of you I can read and write and make music.

Thank you to Laura Barakeris, Gregg Coop, Amanda Lim and Michael Sheehan, my friends and fellow MWG Ink members, for staggering onward joyously with me.

Thank you to my parents, Edwin and Henriette Morelli, who gave me books and pens and music lessons, but most of all love and life.

Thank you to Denis Lacroix, my husband, friend and private librarian, whose love and support helped this book come to fruition.

MEMORY'S DAUGHTER
Alice Major

144 pages
A volume in (cuRRents), a Canadian literature series
978-0-88864-539-5 | $24.95 (T) paper
978-0-88864-765-8 | $19.99 (T) PDF
Poetry / Canadian Literature

WELLS
Jenna Butler

80 pages
Robert Kroetsch Series
978-0-88864-606-4 | $19.95 (T) paper
978-0-88864-525-8 | $15.99 (T) EPUB
978-0-88864-524-1 | $15.99 (T) Amazon Kindle
978-0-88864-792-4 | $15.99 (T) PDF
Poetry / Canadian Literature

DEMETER GOES SKYDIVING
Susan McCaslin

136 pages
A volume in (cuRRents), a Canadian literature series
978-0-88864-551-7 | $19.95 (T) paper
978-0-88864-758-0 | $15.99 (T) PDF
Poetry / Canadian Literature